Cruisers

By John Hamilton

VISIT US AT
WWW.ABDOPUBLISHING.COM

Published by ABDO Publishing Company, PO Box 398166, Minneapolis, MN 55439.
Copyright ©2014 by Abdo Consulting Group, Inc. International copyrights reserved
in all countries. No part of this book may be reproduced in any form without written
permission from the publisher. A&D Xtreme™ is a trademark and logo of
ABDO Publishing Company.

Printed in the United States of America, North Mankato, Minnesota.
112013
012014

 PRINTED ON RECYCLED PAPER

Editor: Sue Hamilton
Graphic Design: Sue Hamilton
Cover Design: John Hamilton
Cover Photo: Corbis
Interior Photos: Alamy-pg 16; American Honda Motor Company-pgs 1, 2-3, 18-19,
20-21 & 28 (bottom); AP-pgs 26-27; Corbis-pgs 4-5, 10-11 & 24-25;
Harley-Davidson Motor Company-pgs 8-9 & 28 (top); Suzuki Motor of
America-pgs 12-13; Triumph Motorcycles-pgs 6-7, 14-15, 22, 23, 29 (top), 30-31 &
32; Thinkstock-pgs 17 & 20 (inset); Yamaha Motor Corporation-pg 29 (bottom).

ABDO Booklinks
Web sites about motorcycles are featured on our Book Links pages. These links are
routinely monitored and updated to provide the most current information available.
Web site: www.abdopublishing.com

Library of Congress Control Number: 2013946162

Cataloging-in-Publication Data

Hamilton, John, 1959-
  Cruisers / John Hamilton.
    p. cm. -- (Xtreme motorcycles)
Includes index.
ISBN 978-1-62403-218-9
1. Motorcycles--Juvenile literature. 2. Motorcycle touring--Juvenile literature.   I.
  Title.
629.227/5--dc23
                                        2013946162

Contents

Ride in Style

Some motorcycles are built for speed and maneuverability. Others are for riding long distances. Cruisers are for riding in style. They are powerful machines that make the heart pound.

About 6 out of 10 motorcycles sold in the U.S. are cruisers.

The 2011 1200 cc Harley-Davidson Sportster is a midsize cruiser.

What are Cruisers?

Cruisers are big, powerful motorcycles. Their engines are rated at 500 cubic centimeters (ccs) and up. Many are rated well over 1,000 ccs. Most cruisers have long chassis and are slung low to the ground. Cruiser owners take great pride in the appearance of their bikes.

Triumph
America

XTREME FACT – Many cruisers are fitted with lots of shiny, attention-getting chrome parts.

Early Cruisers

Today's cruisers are modeled after classic motorcycles of the 1930s through the early 1960s. The most famous of these early machines were built by manufacturers such as Harley-Davidson, Excelsior-Henderson, and Indian.

Harley-Davidson dominated the cruiser category for years. Many people today think of Harley-Davidson when they hear the word "cruiser."

Policemen in Glendale, California, sit on their Harley-Davidson motorcycles in 1930.

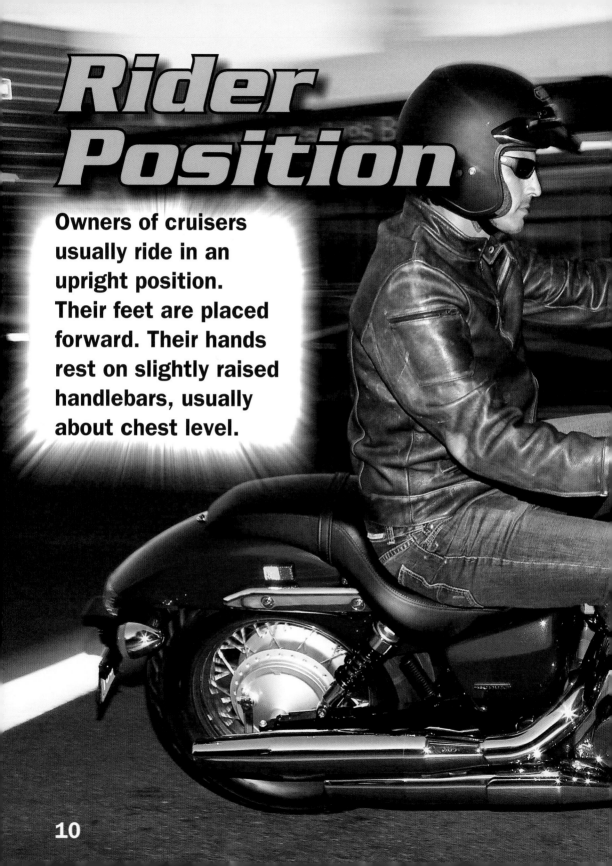

Rider Position

Owners of cruisers usually ride in an upright position. Their feet are placed forward. Their hands rest on slightly raised handlebars, usually about chest level.

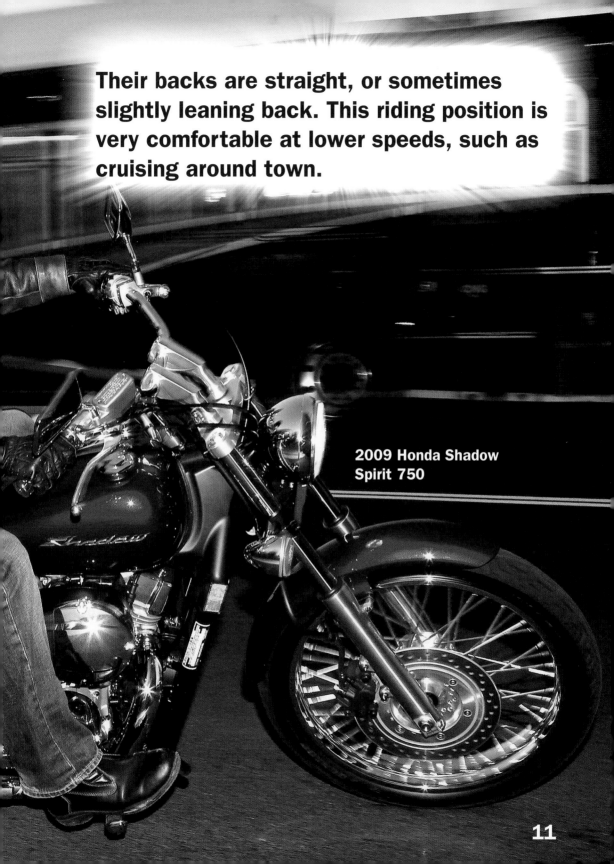

Their backs are straight, or sometimes slightly leaning back. This riding position is very comfortable at lower speeds, such as cruising around town.

2009 Honda Shadow Spirit 750

Engines

Most cruisers have powerful fuel-injected engines. They are easier to start and more efficient than carbureted engines. The most common engine type is the V-Twin. It has two cylinders that are arranged in a "V" shape. Although V-Twins are the most common, other engine types can be found on cruisers, including three- and four-cylinder models.

2013 Suzuki Boulevard C90

V-Twin Engine

Brakes

Cruisers have twin disc brakes, one on the front wheel and one in back. On many motorcycles, the rear brake is smaller. This lessens the chance of it locking up and causing the rider to lose control of the bike.

Triumph America

Rear Brakes:
Single 285mm Disc

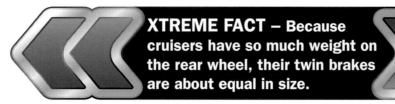

Front Brakes:
Single 310mm Disc

Chassis

Cruisers have long frames, called chassis. They are usually made of heavy steel tubing. Much of the weight is supported in the rear of the bike.

Triumph
Motorcycle
Chassis

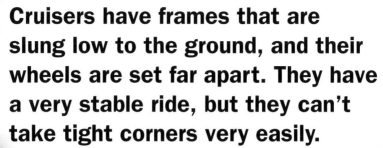

Cruisers have frames that are slung low to the ground, and their wheels are set far apart. They have a very stable ride, but they can't take tight corners very easily.

Suspension

Modern motorcycle suspensions help with road handling and driver comfort.

2007 Honda
Shadow Spirit 750 C2

18

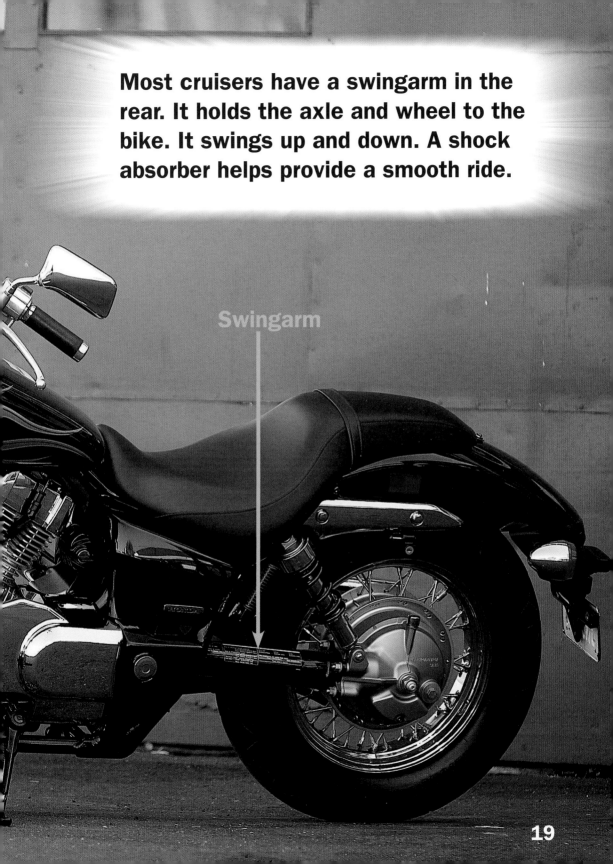

Most cruisers have a swingarm in the rear. It holds the axle and wheel to the bike. It swings up and down. A shock absorber helps provide a smooth ride.

Swingarm

XTREME FACT – Choppers are a kind of customized cruiser. Many choppers have their front forks extended outward.

Honda
2010 Shadow RS

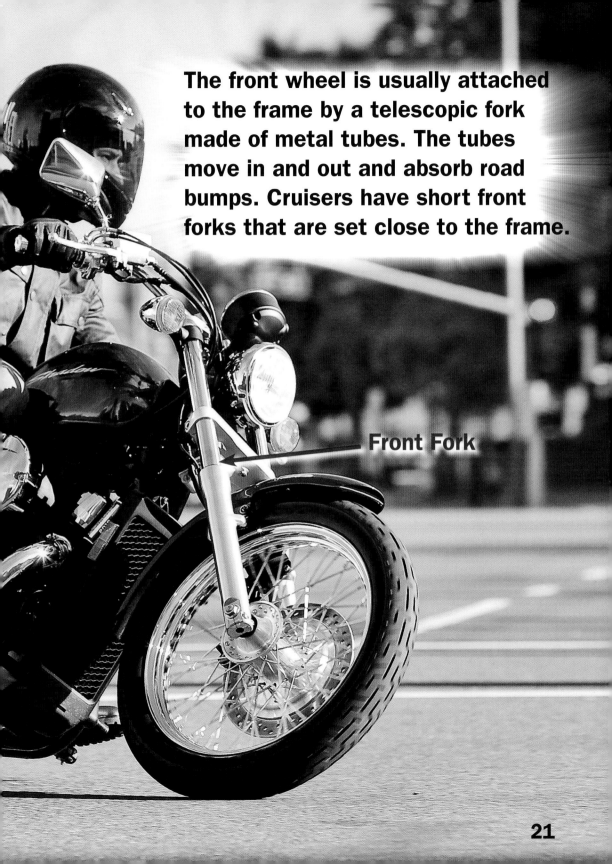

The front wheel is usually attached to the frame by a telescopic fork made of metal tubes. The tubes move in and out and absorb road bumps. Cruisers have short front forks that are set close to the frame.

Front Fork

Baggers

Unlike cruisers, touring motorcycles are meant for traveling long distances in comfort. They are big and powerful. However, many large cruisers are also ridden on cross-country trips. Outfitted with external luggage, they are often called "baggers." They may not be as comfortable as true touring bikes, but they look good rolling down the highway.

Triumph Leather Saddlebag

Triumph
America LT

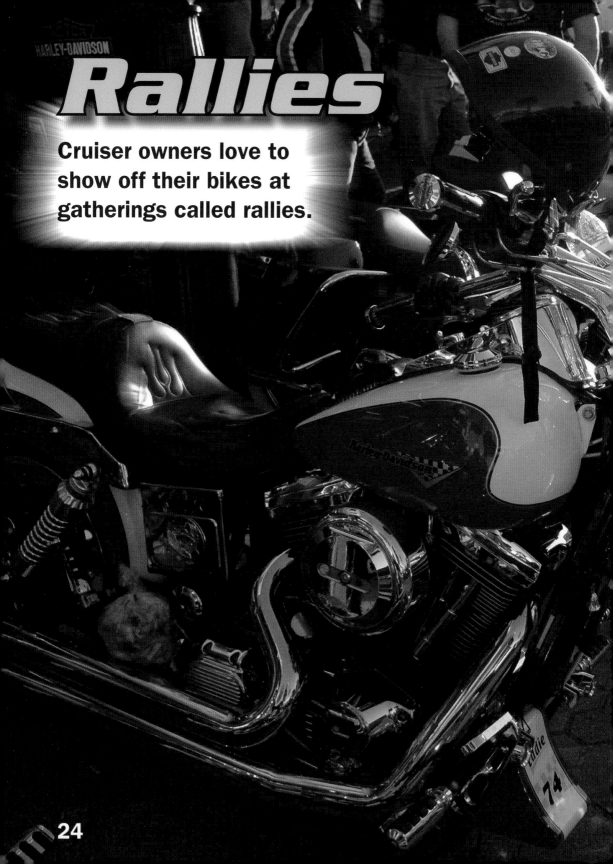

Rallies

Cruiser owners love to show off their bikes at gatherings called rallies.

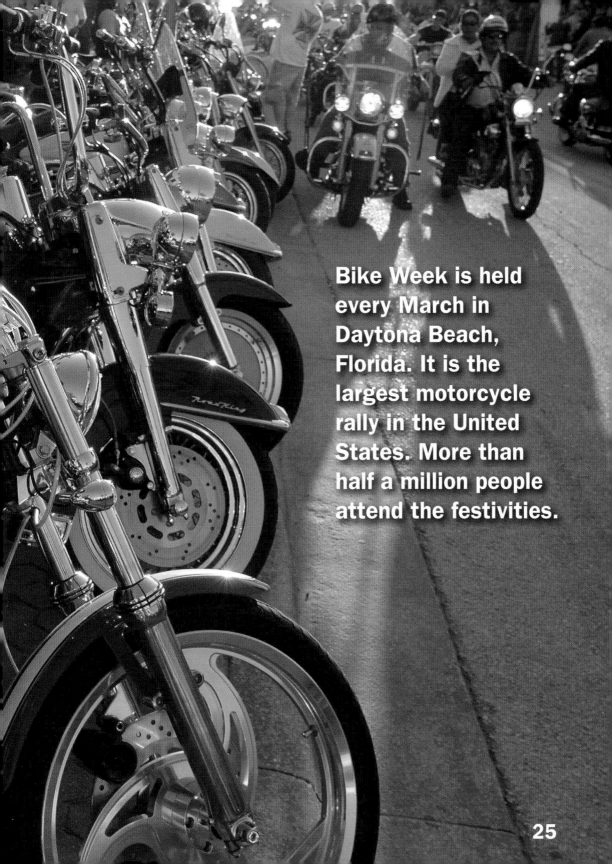

Bike Week is held every March in Daytona Beach, Florida. It is the largest motorcycle rally in the United States. More than half a million people attend the festivities.

WELCOM

Every August, thousands of bikers cruise through the streets of the tiny town of Sturgis, South Dakota. The first Sturgis Motorcycle Rally was held in 1938. Today, rally-goers enjoy watching races, hill climbs, concerts, and many other events. Of course, the main attraction is cruising down Main Street looking good on a hot bike!

Cruiser Showcase

Cruisers are made by many companies including Harley-Davidson, Honda, Triumph, and Yamaha.

Harley-Davidson Sportster XL 1200

Honda Shadow Spirit 750

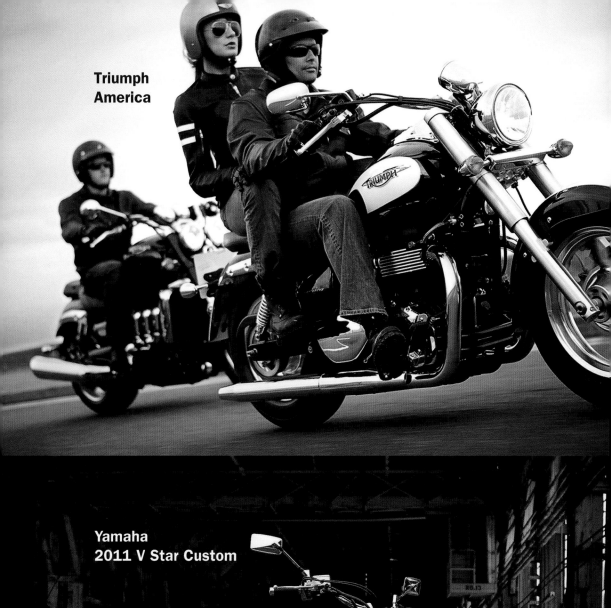

Triumph America

Yamaha 2011 V Star Custom

29

Glossary

CC (Cubic Centimeters)
Engines are often compared by measuring the amount of space (displacement) inside the cylinders where gas and air mix and are ignited to produce power. Displacement is measured in cubic centimeters.

Chassis
The body or frame of a vehicle.

Cylinder
A hollow chamber inside an engine where air and gasoline vapor mix. When ignited by a spark plug, the air/gas mixture explodes, forcing a metal piston inside the cylinder downward. The motion of the piston turns the gears that make the vehicle move.

Fuel-Injected Engine
A system that mixes air and a fine spray of gasoline into an engine cylinder. Instead of using suction to draw in the gasoline, like a carburetor, fuel injection

uses a small nozzle to spray gas under pressure directly into the cylinder. Fuel injection has been widely used on vehicles for more than 30 years. It is generally more efficient than a carburetor, and saves gas.

Maneuverability
To move with skill and ease to a specific location.

Telescopic Fork
A system at the front of a motorcycle where the springs used in the suspension system are hidden inside of metal tubes.

Index